WISDEN The Best

The **40 Leading Cricketers** in the World Today

D0367170

profiles from **Wisden.com**
edited by **Tim de Lisle**
photographs by **Mark Ray**

Acknowledgments

Thanks to many Wisden colleagues for their assistance and acumen:
Tanya Aldred, Sambit Bal, Robin Bevan, Rahul Bhattacharya, Lawrence
Booth, Tom Bowtell, Hugh Chevallier, Christopher Lane, Andrew Miller, Dileep
Premachandran, Camilla Rossiter, Chris Ryan, Rob Smyth, Martin Williamson
and Graeme Wright, and to everyone at Wisden Data Services in Bangalore
for their outstanding player-page statistics, updated ball by ball.

Grateful acknowledgements to *Wisden Cricketers' Almanack*, *Wisden
Cricketers' Almanack Australia*, and the Stats Guru pages at CricInfo.
Any errors can probably not be traced to these sources.

Special thanks to all the writers (see page 62); to Mark Ray for the pictures;
to Steven Lynch for his eagle eye; to Sally Burt for her patience and her
laptop; to Amanda, Daniel and Laura de Lisle for not losing their cool, or
their warmth; and to Nigel Davies, art director of *Wisden Cricket Monthly*,
who didn't so much design the book as make it happen. **TdL**

WISDEN THE BEST © Wisden Online Ltd.
All photographs © Mark Ray, except p8 and p28 © Getty Images

ISBN 0 947766 76 6

Published in 2002 by JOHN WISDEN & CO LTD
13 Old Aylesfield, Golden Pot, Alton, Hampshire, GU34 4BY
E-mail: wisden@wisden.com Website: www.Wisden.com

Printed and bound in Great Britain by Clays Ltd, St Ives plc
Distributed by The Penguin Group
Distributed in Australia by Hardie Grant Books, Melbourne

Photographs by Mark Ray. Designed by Nigel Davies. Copy editing by Steven Lynch

Contents

Introduction

One day, we will look back at the generation of cricketers that played in 2002, and say that they don't make them like that any more. There is genius in the shape of Tendulkar, Warne and Lara; generalship from Steve Waugh, Nasser Hussain and Stephen Fleming; the mystery of Murali and Harbhajan, the might of Kallis, the flair of Gilchrist and Sehwag. There are men who wield the bat like a wand (Martyn, Inzamam) and men who brandish it more like a blunderbuss (Klusener, Hayden). This book, a slim volume designed to accompany a fat book, celebrates them all.

Wisden Cricketers' Almanack is not noted for its omissions, but one thing it doesn't do is pen-portraits. So when we launched Wisden Online in 2000, we made a page for every player who had had a decent international career – 20 Tests or 50 one-dayers. At the centre of the page, acting as an introduction and a jumping-off point into the archives, is either a Wisden obituary, if the player is dead, or a short overview, if he is still with us. We deployed a wide range of writers but only one brief: keep it short, and give us the essence of the player, his distinctive qualities and his place in history, rather than his life story. It is edited versions of a small sample of these overviews that make up this book.

Our subjects are today's top 40 players. In an age that likes to measure the immeasurable, from schools to hospitals, one or two people may have been expecting

Notes

our selection to be done by numbers. It wasn't. The choice was mine, with a lot of help from my friends at Wisden. If you are aghast to find no sign of Andy Caddick, or Mark Boucher, or Sourav Ganguly, you have only myself to blame.

The criterion was simple: sheer excellence. Not career averages, although they were borne in mind, along with strike rates, fielding, and the ability to take a match by the scruff of the neck. We started making lists, and soon reached 45 or 50: getting down to 40 was reassuringly difficult. Like real selectors, we found that the amount of time spent discussing a player was in inverse proportion to his brilliance – Odds-and-Sods' Law, you might call it. Except that in this case even the also-rans were hot stuff. We ended up leaving out a very good team: Michael Slater, Mark Richardson, Hamilton Masakadza, Daryll Cullinan, Mahela Jayawardene, Carl Hooper, Boucher or Kumar Sangakkara, Abdur Razzaq, Daniel Vettori, Jason Gillespie and Caddick. Not to mention Belinda Clark.

We ended up with 11 Australians, and only one West Indian: the story of the past few years. South Africa (with six) came second, as you might expect, equal with India, as you might not – but this exercise was about individuals, not team results, and there were no quotas. If you feel we've got it wrong, or in the unlikely event that we've got it right, let us know with an e-mail to feedback@wisden.com. **TdL**

All statistics are as at February 11, 2002.

Ages are as at April 3, 2002.

Catches are given only for wicket-keepers or notable fielders.

Ⓦ + year = one of Wisden's Five Cricketers of the Year

Ⓦ A + year = Wisden Australia Cricketer of the Year

Abbreviations

RHB, LHB right-hand or left-hand bat

WK wicketkeeper

RF, LF right-arm or left-arm fast bowler

RFM, LFM fast-medium

RM, LM medium-pacer

LBG legbreak and googly bowler

OB offbreak bowler, or offcutters

SLA slow left-arm orthodox

SLC slow left-arm chinaman (wrist spinner)

occ occasional

Steve Waugh

Evolution in action

Australia
RHB, RM

age	36	
Tests	145	
runs	9505 @ 50.83	
wkts	89 @ 35.74	
ct	101	
capt	34	(W24, D5, L5)
ODIs	325	
runs	7569 @ 32.91	
wkts	195 @ 34.67	
ct	111	
capt	106	(W67, L35, T3, NR1)

 1989

 2000-01

Best shot
The back-foot force past cover, played almost level with the stumps

Steve Waugh is the ultimate evolved cricketer. Thrown to the wolves at 20, he flailed at all bowling, sent down bouncers at Viv Richards, and tasted Ashes defeat. Then he helped win a World Cup and made 393 runs before getting out in England in 1989 – but admitted that he did not understand his own game, and 18 months later lost his place to his twin. It was his catharsis. He minimalised his batsmanship, foregoing risk and waiting for the loose ball, which he still punished severely. Forced to bowl less by a bad back, he played a series of epic innings, including 200 in Jamaica in 1994-95 to set up an historic series win, and twin hundreds at Old Trafford to turn the 1997 Ashes. He succeeded Mark Taylor as Test captain in 1999 and began with a torrid 2-2 draw in the Caribbean, but later led Australia boldly to 15 of their world-record 16 Test victories, infecting the team with his own ruthlessness and virtually abolishing the draw. With Shane Warne, he turned Australia around so completely in the 1999 World Cup that they won it. By 2001 he had reinvented one-day cricket too, using attack as the best form of defence, but he lost his job as one-day captain after three bad games against New Zealand in 2002. An inveterate sightseer, he has written a series of popular tour diaries, helped set up a charity for lepers' daughters in Calcutta, and subscribes fervently to the power of the mind. **Greg Baum**

Photo by Tom Shaw, Getty Images

Sachin Tendulkar

The keenest of cricket minds

India
RHB, RM/LBG/OB

age	28
Tests	89
runs	7419 @ 57.96
wkts	25 @ 39.84
ct	60
capt	25 (W4, D12, L9)
ODIs	286
runs	11069 @ 43.92
wkts	105 @ 47.34
ct	92
capt	73 (W23, L43 T1, NR6)

Ⓦ 1997

Top shot
The on-drive from
outside off which is
like a topspin cross-
court forehand

When he became the first man to score 50 international hundreds, Sachin Tendulkar established himself as the greatest of all Indian cricketers. Recognised by Sir Donald Bradman as his modern incarnation, Tendulkar has a skill – a genius – which only a handful have possessed. He was not simply born with it, but developed it by his intelligence and an infinite capacity for taking pains. If there is a secret, it is that Tendulkar has the keenest of cricket minds. At times in a Test series he looks mortal. But he learns every lesson, picks up every cue, dominates the opposing attack sooner or later, and nearly always makes a hundred. His bravery was proved after he was hit on the head on his Test debut in Pakistan, aged only 16; and his commitment to the Indian cause has never been in doubt. The one deficiency, the human weakness, has lain in his response to pressure when second-innings runs have been expected of him. If captaincy – or rather the off-field management of men less skilled than himself – has been beyond him, his reading of the game, and his manifold varieties of bowling, have shown the same acumen. His cricket has been played in the right way, always attacking, and because he knew it was right rather than because he was a child of the one-day age, as he modestly said. The awe of his opponents has matched that of the crowds. The finest compliment is that bookmakers would not fix the odds – or a game – until Tendulkar was out. **Scyld Berry**

Brian Lara

Genius restored

No-one since Bradman has built massive scores as often and as fast as Lara in his pomp. Even his stance was thrilling – the bat raised high in the air, the weight poised on a bent front knee, the eyes low and level. Then the guillotine would fall, sending the ball flashing to the boundary. In the space of two months in 1994, Lara's 375 and 501 not out broke world records for the highest Test and first-class scores, but sudden fame turned him into a confused and contradictory figure. During an inventive but largely fruitless spell as captain of a fading team, Lara reiterated his genius by single-handedly defying the 1998-99 Australian tourists with a sequence of 213, 8, 153 not out and 100. For a while, excess weight and hamstring problems hampered his once-lightning footwork, and the torrent of runs became an occasional spurt. But after Garry Sobers suggested a tweak to his flourishing backlift, Lara returned to his best in Sri Lanka in

West Indies
LHB, LBG

age	32
Tests	83
runs	7221 @ 50.50
ct	107
capt	18 (W6, D2, L10)
ODIs	193
runs	7257 @ 42.44
wkts	4 @ 11.50
ct	82
capt	44 (W20, L23, NR1)

 1995

Best shot
The whip through midwicket off a barely short delivery

2001-02, with 221 and 130 in one Test and 688 runs in the series – 42% of his team's output, another world record. Once again, Lara stands alongside Shane Warne and Sachin Tendulkar as the most charismatic cricketer of the modern era. **Simon Briggs**

Muttiah Muralitharan
Sri Lanka's greatest player

Averaging five and a half wickets per Test, Muttiah Muralitharan is the most successful spinner in the game and the greatest player in Sri Lanka's history. He bowls long spells, yet is forever on the attack. The son of a confectioner from Kandy, Murali has a unique collection of allsorts. From a loose-limbed, open-chested action, his chief weapons are the big-spinning offbreak, the ball that drifts the other way, and the one that goes straight on. With his helicopter wrist, he turns the ball off any surface – someone famously said he would turn it off the M4 motorway – but prefers pitches with bounce. His shyness belies a mental resilience acquired in overcoming prejudice against Tamils in his own country and whispers from abroad that he threw – the consequence of a deformity that stops him straightening his right elbow. In January 2002, aged 29, he became the youngest player to take 400 Test wickets – and the quickest, achieving the feat in only his 72nd Test. If he stays fit and in form, he will break Courtney Walsh's world record of 519 Test wickets some time in 2003. **Simon Wilde**

Sri Lanka
RHB, OB

age	30
Tests	72
runs	703 @ 13.02
wkts	404 @ 23.54
ODIs	183
runs	270 @ 5.63
wkts	267 @ 24.56

 1999

Special delivery
The sharpest offbreak
in the world

Shaun Pollock

Silk and steel

A top-class opening bowler, a batsman capable of scoring Test centuries, a useful slip fielder and now captain of his country, Shaun Pollock is the most complete cricketer since Imran Khan. Loose-limbed and apparently easy-going, Pollock isn't always what he seems. He has a sharp mind, with an impish, laconic streak, and when he had the captaincy thrust upon him under the swirling cloud of match-fixing, any thoughts that he lacked the steel to lead the way out of the abyss were soon dispelled. His elevation seemed to sap some of his pace – Bob Woolmer suggested that he wasn't as svelte as he was – but he continued collecting his wickets at an average of 21 and finally fulfilled the promise of his elegant, upright batting with two blazing hundreds, both made from No. 9. His bowling is a silky blur, delivered stump-to-stump, which gives batsmen nothing except doubts as to which way the ball will seam. His tactical acumen received some harsh notices during the whitewash in Australia in 2001-02, but even if the triple burden eventually proves too much for him, he is sure to be rated as one of the greatest of all South African cricketers. Among his few rivals for that title is his uncle Graeme. **Neil Manthorp**

South Africa
RHB, RFM

age	28	
Tests	63	
runs	2242	@ 31.58
wkts	261	@ 20.72
ct	41	
capt	21	(W9, D7, L5)
ODIs	152	
runs	1571	@ 24.55
wkts	219	@ 22.87
ct	58	
capt	56	(W38, L16, T1, NR1)

Best shot
A cover-drive from the days when batsmen wore caps

Special delivery
Pitches off, jags away, takes the edge

Glenn McGrath
Today's great Australian paceman

Australia
RHB, RFM

age	32
Tests	81
runs	405 @ 6.64
wkts	377 @ 22.01
ODIs	147
runs	84 @ 4.42
wkts	226 @ 23.13

 1998

A 1998-99 and 2001-02

The young Glenn McGrath was described by Mike Whitney as "thin – but Ambrose-thin, not Bruce Reid-thin". Much later, Mike Atherton compared McGrath to Ambrose on a vaster scale. Catapulted from the outback of New South Wales into Test cricket to replace Merv Hughes in 1993, McGrath became, after a faltering start, the great Australian paceman of his time. He bowls an unremitting off-stump line and an immaculate length, gains off-cut and bounce, has a well-aimed bouncer and a well-disguised nip-backer, and adjusts so well to unfamiliar conditions that, from an indifferent start in both countries, he has become as lethal in India and England as he is at Perth or Melbourne. He specialises in the opposition's biggest scalps – especially Atherton's, Brian Lara's and Gary Kirsten's – is unafraid to back himself publicly in these duels, and has shown himself to be unusually durable. He is a batting rabbit who has collected more international wickets than runs but applied himself so intently while playing for Worcestershire that he won a bet with an Australian team-mate by scoring a fifty. Only in his occasional fits of ill-temper does he fail himself. **Greg Baum**

Special delivery
The off-stump lifter that seams away

Shane Warne

Top spinner

Australia	
RHB, LBG	
age	32
Tests	98
runs	1962 @ 16.08
wkts	430 @ 26.73
ct	78
ODIs	175
runs	907 @ 12.77
wkts	268 @ 25.62
ct	72
capt	11 (W10, L1)

Ⓦ 1994

Special delivery
The inswinging,
big-turning legbreak

Shane Warne is one of the few players who can truly be said to have revolutionised cricket. Not only is he the most prolific spin bowler in history, Australia's leading alltime wicket-taker and one of Wisden's Five Cricketers of the 20th Century, but he revived a craft that was almost extinct and made it for a time the most powerful force in the game. No previous wrist-spinner has been at once so prodigious in his drift and turn, so accurate, so mean and so tireless. No previous wrist-spinner has humiliated so many good batsmen. And no previous wrist-spinner has succeeded so handsomely in one-day cricket; all the rest were thought too profligate. Where lesser leggies have the googly, Warne has the flipper, the zooter and the slider. He is also a capable if cavalier lower-order batsman, and latterly a safe fieldsman at first slip. Warne has been as controversial as he has been irresistible, frequently finding himself enmeshed in off-field dramas and even at the periphery of match-fixing. He once said his life felt like a soap opera, and his nickname is Hollywood. His exertions have taken their toll, and surgery on a shoulder and finger seems to have robbed him of some of his old powers. But he remains the single most redoubtable figure in the game today, and his ability to eat Englishmen for breakfast has yet to diminish. **Greg Baum**

Adam Gilchrist

Three players in one

Australia
LHB, WK

age	30
Tests	28
runs	1687 @ 51.12
ct/st	109/9
capt	2 (W1, L1)
ODIs	126
runs	3945 @ 34.01
ct/st	167/30
capt	3 (W3, L0)

Ⓦ 2002

Adam Gilchrist is a three-in-one cricketer who added a dynamic new dimension to an already powerful Australian team when he made a lateish entry into Test cricket in November 1999. He is a dauntless left-hand bat who cuts and pulls what would be good length balls to others, who made three matchwinning Test centuries from No. 7 in his first 20 Tests, who regularly gets Australia off to a flyer in one-day cricket, and briefly held the record for Australia's highest one-day score. He is an acrobatic wicketkeeper, if not yet with Ian Healy's standing-up sophistication, who by force of performance and personality won over doubtful fans after replacing two much-loved incumbents – Tim Zoehrer for Western Australia and Healy for Australia. He is a natural leader who within 12 months of his Test debut was filling in as captain. He is genial, sharp and modern, carrying around a laptop to write his own newspaper columns. It was no coincidence that Australia won all of Gilchrist's first 15 Tests.
Greg Baum

Best shot
The cover-drive
on the up

Jacques Kallis
South African gold

The golden boy of South African cricket, Jacques Kallis has proved just about all there is to prove at the highest level, including fighting a lone hand with the bat, as he did in Australia in 2001-02, and returning a five-wicket haul with the new ball, as he did in Barbados in March 2001. Described by one visiting journalist as "possessing the shoulders of a wildebeest", he is a fearsome prospect with the bat when he decides to cut loose, although more often he settles for being an old-style No. 3 with a textbook defence and a classical cover-drive. As a bowler, he has grown from a part-timer who could keep an end tight by aiming outside off stump into a genuine third seamer capable of high pace, hostility and outswing, although his strike rate remains that of a supporting player. During the few days of the year he spends at home, he can be found in some of Cape Town's trendier bars and restaurants, but the laid-back lifestyle disguises one of the fiercest competitive streaks in the game.
Neil Manthorp

South Africa	
RHB, RFM	
age	26
Tests	57
runs	3787 @ 47.94
wkts	106 @ 29.67
ct	51
ODIs	143
runs	5020 @ 44.42
wkts	132 @ 30.11
ct	61

Best shot
A cover-drive from a 1950s textbook
Special delivery
An equally classical outswinger delivered at high speed

Rahul Dravid

A wall, and a brick

Lovesick women weep for him, but Rahul Dravid is regularly booed to the crease. For he is usually India's No. 3 – destined to bat under a shadow which, though only five foot five, is all-consuming. That his wicket should be so prized by India's own, Tendulkar obsessed, supporters is miserable, because Dravid on song is a batsman of beauty – fluid, wristy, able to dazzle on both sides of the wicket at whim. He can do rigid defence too, which, combined with a chess-player's concentration, has earned him the nickname The Wall, and, increasingly, that is what India's firework display of a middle order needs him to be. But Dravid is more than consistency, more than the dog's howl before the storm. His average is just as handsome overseas as it is on the slow surfaces at home, and he has his own place in history for the commanding 180 he made and the 376 he put on with VVS Laxman which took India to an impossible victory against the Australians at Eden Gardens in March 2001. No-one, not even Sachin, can take that away from him. He remains genial and open, able to live a pretty normal life, as Tendulkar takes the heat of a nation's obsession along with its adoration. Some things are more important than cricket.
Tanya Aldred

India	
RHB, OB, occ WK	
age	29
Tests	53
runs	4257 @ 51.91
ct	60
ODIs	163
runs	5190 @ 37.88
wkts	4 @ 42.50
ct/st	81/4
capt	2 (W2)

Best shot
An artist's off-drive

Andy Flower
Zimbabwe's best player

Zimbabwe
LHB, WK

age	34
Tests	59
runs	4552 @ 53.55
ct/st	147/9
capt	20 (W1, D9, L10)
ODIs	191
runs	5805 @ 33.36
ct/st	135/32
capt	52 (W12, L35, T2, NR3)

 2002

The elder of two Test-playing brothers, Andy Flower has long been Zimbabwe's only batsman of true Test quality in all conditions. In the past two years he has been so phenomenally consistent that he now has no rival as the best player in Zimbabwe's history. His wicketkeeping, though, has been less dependable, and possibly suffered from the added strain of having to lead the side. He has had two stints as captain, leading Zimbabwe to their first Test victory against Pakistan in 1994-95, and then becoming the first Zimbabwean to lead a Test tour of England, in 2000. An assured player of fast bowling since his early days as an opener, Flower has matured into one of the best players of spin in the world, and on the Indian tour early in 2001 he made 540 runs for twice out. By then, he had gone from underrated over-achiever to a recognised star, with a spell at No. 1 in the PwC Ratings. Opposing bowlers targeted him accordingly and after a phenomenal Test against South Africa at Harare, when he made 142 and 199 not out, the highest match tally ever made in a losing cause, he suffered a rare slump. Off the field, Flower is a keen student of Zimbabwe's history – of which he is now a notable part. **Geoffrey Dean**

Best shot
The cover-drive:
half rapier, half shovel

INTERNATIONAL PORTRAIT GALLERY

Our player pages offer vivid sketches of 900 cricketers from the Don to the Turbanator, captured by some of the game's leading writers. Plus fact packs and career stats, updated ball by ball. Coming soon: links to their finest hours, as reported in the Almanack.

WISDEN

www.Wisden.com

24

Graham Thorpe

England's most complete batsman

Graham Thorpe established himself during the winter of 2000-01 as the most complete England batsman since the Gooch-Gower era, able to attack like Alec Stewart – against pace or spin – and to defend like Mike Atherton. Taking the previous winter off was the final step before fulfilment. He had begun as a brilliant counter-attacking left-hander who came off the ropes from the start of his innings to punch a quick 20 and seize the initiative, an invaluable trait. But being the first England player to undergo 10 consecutive years of touring, for the A and Test teams, troubled his back, dulled his edge and gave him a reputation for grumpiness. The winter's rest, and time for reflection with his family, brought him to a peak – as a batsman who enjoyed his cricket again, the best allround fielder in the team, a master of the middle overs of a one-day innings, a contributor in the dressing-room and an occasional captain. The downside came when his marriage fell apart in December 2001, and he had to return home from India in the middle of a Test series.
Scyld Berry

England
LHB, RM

age	32
Tests	70
runs	4583 @ 40.92
ct	74
ODIs	74
runs	2164 @ 37.96
wkts	2 @ 48.50
ct	42
capt	3 (L3)

W 1998

Best shot
The whipped pull
in front of square, front
foot off the ground

Chris Cairns

New Zealand's famous son

New Zealand	
RHB, RFM	
age	31
Tests	54
runs	2830 @ 32.91
wkts	194 @ 28.91
ODIs	146
runs	3530 @ 29.66
wkts	143 @ 33.13
capt	1 (W1)

 2000

Best shot
The dancing
lofted straight drive
Special delivery
A beautifully
concealed slower ball

Some sons of famous fathers wither in the paternal shade. Not Chris Cairns. He was carefully nurtured in the substantial shadow of his father Lance, who in his homespun way had bowled brisk inswingers and destroyed bowlers with a lamp-post disguised as a bat. In fact Cairns senior made sure that his son was coached along classical lines as a bowler of genuine speed, and a batsman of imposing strength and style. Sadly, Chris Cairns's over-eager bowling caused a back injury in his first Test, and he has never been so free or so fast since. However, he could still bowl sharply, move the ball off the seam and deceive with his slower ball, and his batting gained in control. Cairns's aggressive personality was a problem in the mid-1990s when he took on the New Zealand coach Glenn Turner – a move which had Turner sacked and Cairns re-installed by the marketing men as the showpiece and crowd-puller of the New Zealand game. Occasionally, Cairns has lived up to that billing, and his longer innings have been studded with strokes perhaps even more explosive than his father's: the effortless lift over cover, and the powerful pull. A true allrounder, he can take a game by the scruff of the neck with bat or ball – or both, as at The Oval in 1999, when his assault on Phil Tufnell sealed a series victory. But he has suffered a series of knee injuries which have often made him a risk in Test matches while allowing him a fullish one-day career. **Don Cameron**

Anil Kumble

Legspinner with a kick

India
RHB, LBG

age	31
Tests	66
runs	1286 @ 17.86
wkts	300 @ 28.06
ODIs	221
runs	752 @ 10.16
wkts	288 @ 28.94
capt	1 (W1)

🅦 1996

No bowler in India's history has won more Test matches than Anil Kumble, the first Indian spinner to take 300 Test wickets. Cool, calculating, studious and unorthodox, he trades the legspinner's proverbial yo-yo for a spear, as the ball hacks through the air rather than hanging in it, then comes off the pitch with a kick rather than a kink. He does not beat the bat so much as hit the splice, but it's a method that has provided him with stunning success, particularly on Indian soil, where his deliveries burst like grenades on the faintest hint of a crack. He is yet to lead India to a Test victory outside the subcontinent – an indictment of his over-reliance on tailor-made conditions, but also of India's singular dependence on him. Only 106 of his first 300 wickets were taken overseas, at a cost of 39.90 – almost double his average at home (21.55). A big-ripping legbreak would have made Kumble perfect – just like the 10 for 74 he recorded in a single Test innings against Pakistan. In January 2002, in the absence of Ganguly and Dravid, he captained India for the first time in a one-dayer against England, and showed a poise and imagination which put him in line to become India's first bowling captain since Kapil Dev. **Rahul Bhattacharya**

Special delivery
The half-googly that hurries on to middle-and-off

Photo by Tom Shaw, Getty Images

Darren Gough
England's inspiration

Dazzler, extrovert, inspirer, attack leader and England's best strike bowler since Bob Willis and Ian Botham, Darren Gough has steadily grown from often-injured good to match-fit excellent. Not blessed with the height of Curtly Ambrose and Glenn McGrath – and thus lacking a stock ball to match – he has had to develop other means by watching, experimenting and learning. In the process he has become England's first and foremost exponent of reverse-swing and a fine changer of pace. Just as Fred Trueman needed a straight man in Brian Statham to complement him, so has Gough in Andy Caddick. A showman like Dominic Cork, with a softer side, Gough can inspire team-mates and crowds with a diving catch or some daring hitting as well. He has the right chemistry to cause spontaneous combustion, to make things happen and help others play above themselves. Nobody contributed more to England's four series wins in a row in 2000 and 2000-01 than Gough, who was Man of the Series against West Indies and in Sri Lanka. Succeeding there and in Pakistan, the traditional graveyard of fast bowlers, was the final stage of his development. But a poor 2001 Ashes series meant that the final accolade of greatness would not be his. With his benefit in mind, he chose to miss England's Tests in India, and was excluded from the Test squad for New Zealand as a result. **Scyld Berry**

England
RHB, RF

age	31
Tests	56
runs	806 @ 12.40
wkts	228 @ 27.58
ODIs	101
runs	438 @ 10.95
wkts	155 @ 25.57

W 1999

Special delivery
New ball: good-length outswinger. Old ball: inswinging yorker

Inzamam-ul-Haq
Subtlety and strength

Pakistan
RHB, SLA

age	32
Tests	79
runs	5472 @ 46.77
ct	63
capt	1 (L1)
ODIs	254
runs	8218 @ 40.28
wkts	3 @ 21.33
ct	77

Inzamam-ul-Haq has been a symbiosis of strength and subtlety ever since the World Cup semi-final in 1992 when he powered Pakistan to victory over the co-hosts New Zealand by thumping 60 off 37 balls. The power is no surprise, but the sublime touch is remarkable for a man of his bulk. He loathes exercise, often looks a passenger in the field and may have spent more time off the field than any other current player, but with a willow between his palms he is suddenly galvanised. He appears to move slowly, yet always that extra bit of time that marks out the best players. He plays shots all round the wicket, is especially strong off his legs, and unleashes ferocious pulls and lofted drives. Imran Khan has rated him the best batsman in the world against pace. Early on he is vulnerable playing across his front pad or groping outside off stump. He uses his feet well to the spinners although this aggression can be his undoing. Inzi keeps a cool head in a crisis and has succeeded Javed Miandad as Pakistan's premier batsman, but his hapless running between wickets is legendary and often lethal for his partners. He is a safe first slip and outfielder once the ball is within his grasp. **Kamran Abbasi**

Best shot
The turn through square leg – all balance, no effort

Damien Martyn

The invisible man

Australla	
RHB, RM	
age	30
Tests	22
runs	1413 @ 54.35
wkts	1 @ 60.00
ODIs	87
runs	1905 @ 39.69
wkts	11 @ 51.64

W 2002

No contemporary cricketer, Tendulkar aside, makes batting look so simple as Damien Martyn. But it was not always thus. For the brash 21-year-old who waltzed into the Australian team at Dean Jones's expense, batting was an exercise in extravagance. To defend was to display weakness – a policy that backfired in 1993-94 when Martyn's airy square-drive at a crucial moment in Sydney triggered a five-run defeat by South Africa and a seven-year hitch to his own promising career. By the time Western Australia, wanting a pretty face to spearhead their marketing campaign, had made him captain at 23, Martyn looked a tormented man. All the more remarkable, then, that he has blossomed into the relaxed, classical, feathery artist of today. He is an elastic fieldsman, a lively medium-pacer and an old-style batsman whose first movement is back. He plays with a high elbow, a still head, a golfer's deft touch, and has all the shots, including perhaps the most brutal reverse-sweep in the game. Mostly, though, Martyn sticks to the textbook and composes pristine hundreds which, like the feats of the best wicketkeepers, pass almost unnoticed: an observation supported by the curious fact that, despite a Test average in the fifties, he reached the age of 30 without winning a man-of-the-match award. **Chris Ryan**

Best shot
The cover glide, played off the back foot with an upright bat

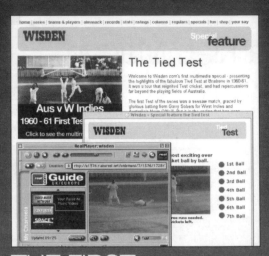

THE FIRST PICTURE SHOW

Eyewitness reports, pictures, archive film footage, audio interviews ... Wisden's multimedia features use all these to bring some of the great moments in cricket history to life. We begin with the 1960 Tied Test, giving you the chance to watch the whole of that pulsating final over and to find out more about a match that lifted the whole game. Look out for more of the same, exclusive to Wisden members.

WISDEN

www.Wisden.com

Ricky Ponting
He knows only attack

Australia
RHB, RM/OB

age	27
Tests	53
runs	3196 @ 43.78
wkts	4 @ 40.00
ct	68
ODIs	131
runs	4800 @ 41.38
wkts	3 @ 34.67
ct	42

Acclaimed by academy coach Rod Marsh as the best teenage batsman he had seen, Ricky Ponting began with Tasmania at 17 and Australia at 20, and was given out unluckily for 96 on Test debut. He was and remains the archetypal modern cricketer: he plays all the shots with a full flourish of the bat and knows only to attack, he bowls sharp medium-pace and occasional offbreaks, and his breathtaking, dead-eye fielding is a force in the game by itself. A gambler and a buccaneer, he is a natural at one-day cricket. He has had his setbacks, against probing seam attacks and high-class finger-spin, which, when out of form, he plays with hard hands. There have been off-field indiscretions that led him to admit publicly to an alcohol problem, but he is part of the heartbeat of one of Australia's most successful teams and after the retirement of Ian Healy he took over as the man who leads the singing of the victory song. With many lessons learned, Ponting is now entering his prime, and his growing maturity was acknowledged by the Australian Cricket Board when he saw off competition from Warne and Gilchrist to succeed Steve Waugh as Australia's one-day captain early in 2002. **Greg Baum**

Special delivery
The pull – hard,
flat and handsome

Allan Donald

White Lightning

South Africa RHB, RF	
age	35
Tests	71
runs	649 @ 10.82
wkts	320 @ 22.10
ODIs	141
runs	88 @ 4.63
wkts	238 @ 31.58

Ⓦ 1992

If the credit for South Africa's success in the modern era could be given to one player, that cricketer would be Allan Donald. A classical action and top-drawer pace would have won him a place in any side in his prime, and for much of his career he was the only world-class performer in the South African team, spearing the ball in, shaping it away and always making things happen. His strike rate is below 50 in Tests and close to 30 in one-day internationals. Inevitably, he was over-bowled, and the injuries began to accumulate in the twilight of his career. Of Afrikaans stock, Donald speaks English with a slight Birmingham accent – at least, to South African ears – picked up during his lengthy spell as Warwickshire's overseas player, a role he filled with distinction. No living South African player, past or present, commands as much respect from the public and his peers as Donald, the first bowler from his country to take 300 Test wickets.
Neil Manthorp

Special delivery
Pitches on off stump
and clips the off bail

Alec Stewart

From touch player to utility man

England
RHB, WK

age	39
Tests	115
runs	7469 @ 39.31
ct/st	220/10
capt	15 (W4, D3, L8)
ODIs	146
runs	4100 @ 31.54
ct/st	136/11
capt	40 (W14, L25, NR1)

W 1993

Best shot

The feathery back-foot cover force

When Stewart is in full flow, there are few who can live with him. Relying on touch, he is in his element against the quicks, cover-driving with a neat flourish and pulling with panache – most memorably when he thundered two centuries in England's storming of Fortress Bridgetown in 1993-94. He is less secure against the spinners, however, and his instinctive style means his career has been a sequence of purple patches and less colourful troughs. Stewart's strength as an opening batsman has been compromised by the selectors' desire for balance: he and Jack Russell swapped the wicketkeeping gloves regularly throughout the 1990s, but Stewart, better standing back than standing up, became the regular No. 1 until he opted out of the 2001-02 tour of India. He took over the England captaincy from Mike Atherton in 1998 and promptly led the side to its first major series win for 12 years, against South Africa. But his leadership was based on passion not nous, and when England lost another Ashes series and flopped in the 1999 World Cup, he was harshly axed. He hit top form again during 2000, and when he scorched a century in his 100th Test, the sheer length of the standing ovation he received suggested that Stewart had become a national institution. He remained a pivotal figure in the England side, batting at No. 5 or even 6, until the decision to take a rare break in 2001-02 threatened to pension him off. **Lawrence Booth**

Wasim Akram

In our dreams

A dream allrounder. At his best Wasim Akram plays like most of us would wish to. He has complete mastery over swing and seam, and sometimes moves the ball both ways in one delivery. All this comes at high speed from a quick, ball-concealing action, and is backed up by the threat of a dangerous bouncer or deceptive slower delivery. Wasim is rated by many as the best left-arm fast bowler of all time and his career record, spanning 860 international wickets, bears that out – along with the high regard of his contemporaries. He hits the ball like a kicking horse, but batsmanship is one skill in which Wasim has underachieved since announcing himself with a stylish hundred at Adelaide in 1989-90. Charming and charismatic if not greatly inclined to analysis, he was the natural successor to Imran Khan as Pakistan's leader and captain, but the match-fixing controversies of the 1990s harmed him, blunting his edge and dimming his lustre. **Kamran Abbasi**

Pakistan
LHB, LFM

age	35
Tests	104
runs	2898 @ 22.64
wkts	414 @ 23.62
capt	25 (W12, D5, L8)
ODIs	323
runs	3359 @ 16.15
wkts	446 @ 23.86
capt	109 (W 66, L41, T2)

Best shot
A cracking cover drive
Special delivery
The full-length inswinger that reverses into a vicious late outswinger

Waqar Younis
Reversing fast

Pakistan RHB, RF		
age	30	
Tests	78	
runs	851 @ 10.25	
wkts	352 @ 22.66	
capt	7	(W6, L1)
ODIs	223	
runs	855 @ 10.96	
wkts	358 @ 23.50	
capt	23	(W17, L6)

W 1992

The man who really put the reverse into swing. Waqar Younis bucked the 1980s trend of bowling fast and short by bowling fast and full. Not an obvious recipe for success until you factor in prodigious late inswing, designed to smash into the base of leg stump or the batsman's toes. In his youth, he was one of the fastest ever. Waqar's surging run is a glorious sight – and an incredible strain on his body. His method of aiming for the stumps rather than the batsman has earned him the best strike rate of any bowler with 200 Test wickets. It could have been even better: back injuries cut short his prime, but determination has always resurrected him, although he is easily pushed over the line that divides aggression and intimidation and has been known to attract the referee's attention with his work on the ball. Lusty blows are his batting staple, but Waqar bats with the air of a man who thinks he can do better. An unexpected choice as captain in his dotage, he made an almost immediate success of the job, stealing a victory at Old Trafford and then winning six Tests in a row when world politics allowed Pakistan to take the field. By uniting and galvanising the disparate talents at his disposal, he also repaired Pakistan's one-day form. **Kamran Abbasi**

Special delivery
The definitive toe-crusher

Gary Kirsten
Grit incarnate

South Africa
LHB, OB

age	34
Tests	80
runs	5479 @ 42.15
wkts	2 @ 70.50
ct	70
capt	1 (W1)
ODIs	170
runs	6414 @ 41.12
ct/st	58/1

Long gone are the days of Gary Kirsten the Man's Man, partying and playing the bachelor for all it was worth. Blissfully married to Deborah and living under the shadow of Table Mountain in Cape Town, Kirsten is now the softly spoken voice of reason. Yet he remains one of the most grittily determined opening batsmen in the world. Kirsten makes a habit of proving his critics wrong, never more so than when equalling Daryll Cullinan's national Test record score of 275 against England at Durban in 1999-2000. after he had apparently been selected on a last-chance basis. Few cricketers practise harder and few in their thirties are fitter. On debut against Australia in 1993-94 he was soon confronted with two gullies and a backward point, such were the limitations of his strokeplay. But after spending hundreds of hours in the nets and the gym, he now drives as straight as anyone, and whips deliveries on off stump through midwicket in the first 15 overs of one-day matches. **Neil Manthorp**

Best shot
A lumberjack's cut

Mark Waugh
More style than guile

Australia RHB, OB	
age	36
Tests	122
runs	7780 @ 42.51
wkts	57 @ 40.00
ct	167
ODIs	244
runs	8500 @ 39.35
wkts	85 @ 34.55
ct	108

 1991

Mark Waugh will always be set apart by the fact that he is one of the only pair of twins to have played Test cricket, by the fact that his first game, against England in 1990-91, was at his brother's expense, and by his sublime batsmanship, evident in his debut century in that Adelaide match and in many memorable innings since. Though he can play all the shots effortlessly, the prince of them is a drive to leg, followed by a stroke that is more caress than cut. Waugh was once an aggressive medium-pacer who opened New South Wales's bowling, is now a respectable offspinner, and has always been a breathtaking fieldsman who takes impossible catches at second slip as if with a butterfly net. At Lord's in 2001 he broke Mark Taylor's world Test record of 157 catches by a non-wicketkeeper. Admiration of Waugh is qualified by a history of succumbing to unworthy shots, which means his Test average is nearer to 40 than 50. In this, he is the antithesis of his twin, though he maintains he is a victim of appearances. He is a guileless man whose only real brush with controversy was to have opened his door to the knocking of bookmakers. **Greg Baum**

Best shot

An on-drive to rival Greg Chappell and Peter May

Saeed Anwar
Gracefully compelling

Pakistan
LHB, SLA

age	33
Tests	55
runs	4052 @ 45.53
ODIs	230
runs	8348 @ 39.75
wkts	5 @ 35.20

W 1997

Majestic timing and placement are Saeed Anwar's hallmarks. He is an opener capable of electrifying starts in all cricket through graceful strokeplay rather than brute force. He loves driving through the off side with minimal footwork. He annihilates any bowler offering width outside off stump, rocking back to cut anything fractionally off-target, although he can also fall into the left-hander's trap of guiding the ball straight into the hands of fourth slip or gully. He first came to prominence as a one-day player but soon achieved equal success in Test cricket, and has always been capable of making big scores fast even without a settled partner. Saeed's fielding is weak, he is injury-prone, and his footwork has become less assured. But he still holds the record for the highest score in one-day internationals and at his best he remains one of the most gracefully compelling players on the international stage. Mike Atherton, on being told once that he had been preferred to Anwar in a World XI chosen by readers of *Wisden Cricket Monthly*, said: "I know who I'd rather watch." **Kamran Abbasi**

Best shot
A dashing, flashing cut

Matthew Hayden

Power and willpower

Strength is Matthew Hayden's strength – both mental and physical. It has enabled him to shrug off career-long carping that he is technically too limited for Test cricket because of the way he plays around his front pad. Before his maiden first-class innings, he asked if anyone had made 200 on debut, then went out and hit 149. The runs have not abated since. Tall, powerful and equipped with concentration befitting the triathlete, fisherman and surfer that he is, he batters the ball at and through the off side for days at a time. He has made himself reliable in the slips and gully, and is good for a relieving spell of medium-pace. His earliest Test matches were exclusively against South Africa and West Indies, a trial for any opener. They were not auspicious, but patience and willpower have latterly won the day, especially in India in 2000-01 where he slog-swept his way to 549 runs, an Australian record for a three-Test series. By the end of 2001 he had broken Bob Simpson's Australian record for most Test runs in a calendar year and formed a prodigiously prolific opening partnership with Justin Langer. **Greg Baum**

Australia LHB, RM	
age	30
Tests	27
runs	2045 @ 47.56
ct	25
ODIs	29
runs	808 @ 32.32
ct	11

Best shot
The thwack through the covers

Justin Langer
Wooden, watchful and workmanlike

Justin Langer was struck such a fearful blow to the helmet by Ian Bishop in his first Test innings in 1992-93 that for a while he was seeing double while facing West Indies. Since then, nothing has seemed too hard. He remained a bit player for Australia until finally seizing the No. 3 spot, which had been vacant since David Boon's retirement. His technique is wooden, watchful and workmanlike, built around the cut and square-drive. With it, though, Langer has demonstrated an ability to compile huge scores, and sometimes to score astonishingly quickly; in New Zealand in 1999-2000, he made what was then Australia's third-fastest Test century, and after losing his place to Damien Martyn in 2001, he returned as a hard-hitting opener and made five hundreds in seven Tests against three different opponents. He also succeeded Boon at short leg, where he sometimes shows too much courage for his own good. Langer is Australia's Samuel Pepys, keeping a daily internet diary while on tour. **Greg Baum**

Australia
LHB

age	31
Tests	48
runs	3364 @ 44.85
ct	32
ODIs	8
runs	160 @ 32.00
ct/st	2/1

 2001

Best shot
The well-judged
nudge past gully

VVS Laxman

From the sublime to the frustrating

India	
RHB	
age	27
Tests	29
runs	1703 @ 37.02
ct	40
ODIs	32
runs	681 @ 24.32
ct	15

 2002

At his sublime best, VVS Laxman is a sight for the gods. Wristy, willowy and sinuous, he can match, and sometimes better, Sachin Tendulkar for strokeplay. His on-side game is comparable to his idol Mohammad Azharuddin, and yet he is decidedly more assured on the off side, as long as he remembers not to waft towards the two gullies that often greet him. In March 2001, all the dreams he had had as a wannabe medical student came true when he tormented Steve Waugh's then-invincible Australians with a majestic 281 at Calcutta – one of the greatest performances of all time. He made three other fifties in that series, and 289 runs at an average of 57 in the one-dayers: consistency at last. But then he went back to mortality, and even though he continued to produce some breathtaking strokes there was a breathlessness about his batting and he seemed to settle for the frustrations of the 20s and 30s. Laxman has not been helped by whimsical selectors, who made him open the batting for more than two years, and dropped him from the one-day side in January 2002 when his one-day figures had improved in the previous year. Still, he could not argue with their point: he must put a higher price on his wicket. It's unlikely he will ever scale the heights of that 281 again, but if he even gets close, Indian cricket will have been well served. And he has it in him to be captain, as well as one of India's best slip catchers. **Sambit Bal**

Best shot
The back-foot glide through the covers

45

Marcus Trescothick

A senior player since day one

There is something biblical about Marcus Trescothick's career: seven years of plenty as a schoolboy, seven years of famine when he reached the Somerset 1st XI. And lo, it came to pass in 1999 that he batted on a pacey pitch at Taunton against Glamorgan while Duncan Fletcher was their coach, and made a storming 167, with five sixes, when the next-best score was 50. When England needed a stand-in one-day opener in 2000, Fletcher remembered Trescothick. He took to international cricket like a duck to a TV screen. A true opener, he formed a habit of starting a series well with a mixture of expert leaves, crisp cover-drives, spanking pulls and fearless slog-sweeps. Hefty, knock-kneed and genial, he is described by Nasser Hussain as a left-handed Gooch, but his ease on the big stage and his blazing one-day strokeplay are just as reminiscent of David Gower. His first four England hundreds came in a losing cause, confirming his ability to keep his head while all around are losing theirs. Opening in Tests with Mike Atherton, Trescothick acquired the air of a senior player as if by osmosis, joined the management committee on his first tour, and soon became Hussain's heir apparent – while admitting that he did not know what sort of captain he would be. All that stands between him and the top drawer is a tendency to get out when well set, and the management's inclination to throw him the wicketkeeping gloves. **Tim de Lisle**

England
LHB, RM, occ WK

age	26
Tests	19
runs	1311 @ 38.56
wkts	1 @ 52.00
ct	15
ODIs	32
runs	1201 @ 38.74
wkts	2 @ 22.50
ct	9
capt	1 (W1)

Best shot
The punched drive past extra cover

Chaminda Vaas

Sri Lanka's greatest seamer

Sri Lanka LHB, LFM		
age	28	
Tests	58	
runs	1288 @ 19.52	
wkts	190 @ 28.82	
ODIs	175	
runs	1079 @ 14.20	
wkts	218 @ 27.39	

Chaminda Vaas has served Sri Lanka extremely well with intelligent left-arm new-ball bowling. He is easily the most penetrative and successful paceman they have had, and their only realistic match-winning bowler after Murali. He rarely finds home pitches to his liking but seams and swings the ball with skill, his trademark ball being the late indipper. Vaas outbowled New Zealand's seamers in green conditions at Napier to give Sri Lanka their first win in an overseas Test, in 1994-95, and after a solid few years, he made a quantum leap in 2001-02, taking 26 wickets in the 3-0 rout of West Indies and joining Imran Khan as the only fast bowlers ever to have taken 14 wickets in a match in the subcontinent. Within a week he had added the first eight-for ever taken in a one-day international – 8 for 19 against Zimbabwe, who were shot out for 38. Strongly built, he is an effective lower-order hitter. He is believed to have the longest set of forenames (49 characters) and one of the shortest surnames (four characters) of any Test cricketer. **Simon Wilde**

Special delivery
The classic
left-armer's
in-curler

Harbhajan Singh

Rebel turned world-beater

Harbhajan Singh embodies the spirit of the new Indian cricketer. His arrogance and cockiness – traits that earned him a rebuke from the establishment and suspension from the National Cricket Academy – translate into self-belief and passion on the cricket field, and Harbhajan has the talent to match. With a whiplash action, remodelled after he was reported for chucking, he exercises great command over the ball, has the ability to vary his length and pace, and can turn it the other way. His main wicket-taking ball, however, is the one that climbs wickedly on the unsuspecting batsman from a good length, forcing him to alter his stroke at the last second. In March 2001, it proved too much for the all-conquering Australians as Harbhajan collected 32 wickets in three Tests while none of his team-mates managed more

India	
RHB, OB	
age	21
Tests	20
runs	255 @ 12.75
wkts	81 @ 29.22
ODIs	40
runs	194 @ 11.41
wkts	54 @ 27.46

Special delivery
The drifter that bounces and turns towards slip

than three. Purists might mutter about his lack of loop and flight, but this was one of the greatest performances ever by a finger-spinner – at a time when orthodox offspin was supposed to be history. **Sambit Bal**

Brett Lee

21st-century boy

Australia RHB, RF	
age	25
Tests	18
runs	357 @ 25.50
wkts	74 @ 24.82
ODIs	34
runs	159 @ 14.45
wkts	58 @ 25.16

If Brett Lee was a Ferrari ... No. There is no if. He is already the fastest in the world, equal with Shoaib Akhtar at 156-157 kph, and has the strike rate to be one of the greats. When he releases the throttle and begins that smooth acceleration, the spectator stays his drinking hand. The leaping, classical delivery may produce a devastating yorker, a devilish slower ball or a young-Donald outswinger. Add a dash of peroxide, a fruity vocabulary, a trademark jump for joy, a stylish bat (he averages more with it than with the ball), a streak of sadism when bowling at tailenders, a pop group (Six And Out), and an endearing dedication to a day job at a gentleman's outfitters, and you have the 21st century's first designer cricketer – not to mention a priceless pin-up boy. Australia just have to count the children in Brett Lee shirts to know his value, and Steve Waugh has nurtured him well – the unruly incisor to McGrath's molar. It hasn't all been easy: Lee has struggled against accusations of throwing and stress fracture after stress fracture, and he had a strangely meagre first Ashes series. But already he seems naked without the baggy green cap – and the world's best team seems a little less fearsome without him. **Tanya Aldred**

Special delivery
The outswinger that jags back to hit off

Virender Sehwag
The world's most exciting young batsman

India
RHB, OB

age	23
Tests	4
runs	235 @ 47.00
ct	5
ODIs	28
runs	699 @ 30.39
wkts	13 @ 46.46
ct	6

Best shot
The gentle push
that races past the
cover sweeper

Virender Sehwag is a bundle of talent and aggression, and a cricketer who makes things happen. In his first Test innings, at Bloemfontein in 2001-02, he came in at 68 for 4 on a greentop and made a ravishing hundred, adding 220 with his hero and lookalike Sachin Tendulkar. In his second Test, he was had up for excessive appealing by the match referee Mike Denness, convicted on three counts and banned for one Test – the earliest in a career that anyone had ever been banned. His third Test was not a Test at all because the Indian board, feeling (as many did) that Denness had over-reacted, insisted on picking him. As the world game threatened to split in two, Sehwag became cricket's biggest political football since Basil D'Oliveira. His career could have been blighted, but when he returned after finally serving his sentence, his back-foot drives, late cuts and whips to leg soon banished all thoughts of politics and confirmed him as the world's most exciting batsman under 25. His ability to hit respectable deliveries for four is such that the Indian selectors were prepared to break up the massively prolific one-day opening partnership between Tendulkar and Sourav Ganguly. Sehwag celebrated by scoring his runs against England in 2002 at more than one a ball. When he adds a drop of discretion to his game, he will be a star.
Tim de Lisle

Nasser Hussain

Captain dynamic

Brought up by his Indian-born, Essex-based coach of a father with the ambition to represent England, Nasser Hussain's desire was such that he was prepared to forego his natural style – opening the face of the bat, running the ball to third man – to succeed at Test level. His success was a triumph of willpower over several technical deficiencies including a dominant bottom hand and unorthodox leg and head positions which led him to lean back in the drive. Since taking

England	
RHB, captain	
age	34
Tests	66
runs	3726 @ 35.15
ct	46
capt	27 (W10, D8, L9)
ODIs	60
runs	1581 @ 31.00
ct	32
capt	28 (W17, L11)

Top shot
The twinkle-toed lofted on-drive that tells the spinners who's boss

over from Alec Stewart in July 1999, Hussain has established himself as the best and – not coincidentally – the most articulate England captain since Mike Brearley. Under Hussain, England won four Test series in a row for the first time since Brearley, and rose to third place in the ICC Test Championship, after being ninth and last in the prototype Wisden World Championship in September 1999. Hussain's style of captaincy has been a reflection of his personality, never static, always full of energy and ideas. He has been known to make four field-changes in one over in a Test match, searching for the solution, trying to make up for the lack of variety among his attack with imaginative placements. His batting while captain has veered from the heights of England's tour to South Africa to a worse run than even Brearley knew. Yet so widely admired was his captaincy that his place was never questioned, unlike Brearley's. Nor were there any calls for his head after the Ashes drubbing that had done for many of his predecessors. A firebrand in his youth, renowned for looking after number one in run-out situations, Hussain has tempered his fire into a fierce commitment to England's cause – when his brittle fingers aren't broken. He has also shared the quality of the finest captains in being lucky, not with the toss, but in the arrival of central contracts and Duncan Fletcher as coach. **Scyld Berry**

WHEN 154 BEAT 333

The Wisden 100 is a computer ranking of the very best international performances. Out of 55,000 Test innings, Graham Gooch's 154 comes in at No. 3. Find out why it rates higher than his 333, and browse the top 100s for batting and bowling in both Tests and one-day internationals. Clue: in the Test bowling, a man with five wives is top.

WISDEN

www.Wisden.com

Stephen Fleming
Youthful veteran

New Zealand LHB		
age	29	
Tests	65	
runs	3898 @ 37.48	
ct	95	
capt	41	(W15, D13, L13)
ODIs	165	
runs	4484 @ 30.71	
wkts	1 @ 28.00	
ct	76	
capt	105	(W39, L58, T1, NR7)

Promoted to the New Zealand captaincy as a still-immature 23-year-old after the sacking of Lee Germon, Fleming has grown slowly into the role. An outstanding teenage batsman, he had only three years at Test level before becoming New Zealand's youngest captain. His promotion coincided with the selection of the Australian-born Steve Rixon as New Zealand coach and the development of a management structure which tended to diminish the captain's influence in team practices and policies. A free stroker of the ball who takes a special delight in the straight-drive, Fleming tends to make runs when his team needs them but not always enough of them: only three of his first 35 Test fifties turned into hundreds. In 2000-01 Fleming demanded, and got, a stronger hand in running his team. A year later he shrewdly put the skids under the Australians on their own turf and almost became the first visiting captain to win a series there since Richie Richardson with West Indies in 1992-93. Just reward for a man who is now New Zealand's most successful captain in terms of Test wins. He is also, following the sacking of Steve Waugh from the one-day team – which was largely engineered by New Zealand – the only captain from the 1999 World Cup who is still in the job. **Don Cameron**

Top shot
A resounding straight-drive

Michael Bevan

The definitive finisher

Australia
LHB, SLC

age	32
Tests	18
runs	785 @ 29.07
wkts	29 @ 24.24
ODIs	171
runs	5635 @ 56.92
wkts	36 @ 45.97

Every turn in Michael Bevan's career has been a contradiction. He found batting simple to the point of boring in making a debut first-class century while still an academy student, was nominated to succeed Allan Border in Australia's middle order, yet twice was bounced out of Test cricket by unprepossessing England. His mark in Tests remains a matchwinning 11-wicket bag while bowling his mercurial left arm wrist-spinners at West Indies at Adelaide in 1996-97. Instead, he has become the world's best one-day batsman, with a game built on a sublime instinct for gaps, Olympian speed between the wickets and a survival instinct so well honed that he collects a not-out every third innings. His ability to take charge in the last 20 overs is such that when cricket people talk about a "finisher", they mean Bevan. He is sure in the field, but less dynamic since a shoulder injury. He has also scored prolifically for New South Wales, Yorkshire and Sussex, and has joined Leicestershire for 2002. **Greg Baum**

Best shot
The late force past the man at backward point

Jonty Rhodes
Leader in his field

South Africa RHB		
age	32	
Tests	52	
runs	2532 @ 35.66	
ct	34	
ODIs	220	
runs	5212 @ 34.29	
ct	97	

 1999

Best shot

The slog-sweep that is more of a baseball swing

The Jonty Rhodes legend may have begun with the diving run-out of Inzamam-ul-Haq during the 1992 World Cup, but it would never have grown as it did without genuine substance. Rhodes works harder than anyone else in a team of hard workers, frequently delaying the team bus at the end of practice for one more round of reflex catches. Nobody has ever fielded better in the key one-day position of backward point, where he leaps like a salmon, throws off balance, and stops singles by reputation alone. He labours just as hard over his batting which needed, and underwent a complete technical overhaul in 1997 – whereupon he averaged 50 for the rest of his Test career, until he gave it up to concentrate on one-day cricket in 2000. Few batsmen have turned the quick single into a finer art form, and his willingness to experiment and adapt saw him lead the way with the reverse-sweep under Bob Woolmer's tutelage. But Rhodes is just as likely to delay the bus by relentlessly signing autographs for gaggles of persistent children; the arrival of his own, a daughter, was instrumental in his semi-retirement. Indeed, Rhodes may have become the first cricketer to claim paternity leave. Rightly, there is give and take in Rhodes's life. He has more endorsements than any team-sport player in South Africa's history, and is constantly exploring the boundaries and horizons of commerce.
Neil Manthorp

Lance Klusener

A refined slugger

South Africa
LHB, RM/OB

age	30
Tests	48
runs	1904 @ 33.40
wkts	78 @ 37.49
ODIs	129
runs	2844 @ 41.82
wkts	155 @ 28.29

 2000

Few would figure Lance Klusener to be a No. 11, but that's where he batted after breaking into first-class cricket as a fast bowler. A childhood spent among Zulu children on a sugar-cane farm and three years in the army contributed to a straightforward approach to bowling: hit the batsman's head if you can't hit his stumps. He spent a couple of years bowling just two lengths before a serious ankle injury in 1998 forced him to drop his pace and develop further skills. Around 2000 he began fulfilling the role of second spinner, bowling medium-pace cutters off just six paces that many batsmen find impossible to score from. Few would pencil Klusener in at the top of the order either, especially after his dismal form in West Indies (2000-01) and Australia (2001-02). But contrary to his reputation as an unrefined slogger, set in stone at the 1999 World Cup, Klusener is one of the most skilled players in the game – which makes him one of the most adaptable. While his heavy bat sends the ball arcing to all fields, he is introspective by nature and happiest holding a fishing rod. Not talking to the media is another hobby of his, although when he breaks his silence he does so with quiet intelligence and impressive clarity of thought. **Neil Manthorp**

Best shot
The club past extra cover (or midwicket)

Special delivery
The booming full-length inswinger

Sanath Jayasuriya

Gently brutal

Sri Lanka
LHB, SLA

age	32
Tests	69
runs	4339 @ 41.32
wkts	65 @ 32.22
capt	31 (W15, D7, L9)
ODIs	252
runs	7235 @ 30.79
wkts	214 @ 34.93
capt	70 (W44, L24, T1, NR1)

 1998

One of the world's most uncompromising strikers of the ball, Sanath Jayasuriya found belated fame as a pinch-hitter at the 1996 World Cup, kick-starting Sri Lanka all the way to the trophy and changing the nature of the one-day game, in Asia at least, for years to come. Then he set about demonstrating that he was also capable of massive scoring in Tests. He remains dizzily dangerous, especially on the subcontinent's slower, less bouncy surfaces, but uncertainty entered his five-day game after he succeeded the formidable Arjuna Ranatunga as Sri Lanka's captain in 1999. Short of stature and powerfully built, he cuts and pulls with awesome force, his brutal bat-wielding at odds with his shy, gentle nature. Wised-up opponents have learned to set traps in the gully to stem the flow of runs through this, a favourite area for him as for so many left-handers. But he has become correspondingly more effective as an orthodox left-arm spinner, and his unfussy captaincy has steered Sri Lanka to third place in the world order. **Simon Wilde**

Best shot
A lofted cut
like a rocket

Saqlain Mushtaq
International man of mystery

Pakistan RHB, OB	
age	25
Tests	38
runs	748 @ 15.91
wkts	165 @ 28.86
ODIs	147
runs	658 @ 12.19
wkts	262 @ 20.84

 1998

A new-age offspinner who loves variation, Saqlain Mushtaq has mastered a mystery ball that spins away from the batsman even though it is delivered with an offspinner's action. He calls it the doosra, Urdu for the other one. He has a fast, short-stepping action with a halting delivery, and has a propensity to bowl no-balls, unusually for a bowler with such a short run. Saqlain has been criticised for attempting too much variation and he often throws in the doosra the first time a batsman faces him. He was the fastest bowler ever to 100 one-day wickets, and a mark of his control is that he regularly bowls at the death. His strike rate is a modest 70 in Tests, but a sensational 29 in one-day internationals, and he is lethal in county cricket with Surrey. He has adhesive qualities as a batsman, but struggles to get the ball off the square. Nonetheless he has shared several valuable lower-order stands and has even made a dogged Test hundred.
Kamran Abbasi

Special delivery
The doosra – a fully-fledged legbreak with no discernible change of action

Contributors

And the best day's cricket they have seen

Tim de Lisle, 39, is editor of Wisden.com. He was an Editor of the Year in 1999 with *Wisden Cricket Monthly*. He is pop critic of the *Mail on Sunday* and cricket columnist for the *Independent*. "Australia v South Africa, the 1999 World Cup semi-final at Edgbaston: the perfect one-day match, a tie with a savage twist, and several great players at their best."

Kamran Abbasi, 33, is a Lahore-born, London-based doctor turned journalist. He is a columnist for *Wisden Cricket Monthly, Wisden Asia Cricket* and Wisden.com, and assistant editor of the *British Medical Journal*. "Headingley, 1999. Inzi lays into McGrath, Shoaib bowls Steve Waugh, and Pakistan's fans make it a day to remember after years of angst at that ground. And the Aussies were all but out of the World Cup. Sweet while it lasted."

Tanya Aldred, 29, is assistant editor of Wisden.com and a contributor to the *Guardian*. "England v West Indies, 2000. Because Lord's exploded, and Cork did too. Because Ambrose and Walsh never gave up. Because 13 members of my family counted down every run. And because the chocolate fingers didn't run out."

Sambit Bal, 34, is editor of *Wisden Asia Cricket* magazine and Wisden.com India, and former editor of Total-Cricket.com and *Gentleman* magazine. "The final day of India v Pakistan, Chennai 1999. It was riveting, stirring, wrenching and uplifting. From 82 for 5, Tendulkar, fighting a bad back and a top-quality attack, took India to 254, then they collapsed to 258 all out, to lose by 12 runs. An entire stadium rose to salute the Pakistanis. All was well with cricket and the world."

Greg Baum, 42, is senior sports writer for the *Age* in Melbourne. He was its cricket correspondent 1993-1998. "Adelaide, January 1993. Australia came within the thickness of Craig McDermott's batting glove of snatching their first series win against the West Indies for nearly 20 years. Courtney Walsh took the last wicket with one run needed and said he never doubted he would take it. Australia lost both match and series, but never their sense of hurt."

Scyld Berry, 47, has been cricket correspondent of the *Sunday Telegraph* since 1993. He did the same job for *The Observer* 1978 to 1989, and is on the Editorial Board of *Wisden Cricket Monthly*. "The most memorable, but not pleasurable, day will always be the last day of England's Test at Kingston in 1985-86. On a broken pitch, Marshall and Patterson bowled as quickly and dangerously as human beings can ever have bowled – and it wasn't televised."

Rahul Bhattacharya, 22, is a staff writer with Wisden.com and *Wisden Asia Cricket*. "Australia v South Africa at Headingley, 1999 World Cup. The semi-final at Edgbaston was special too, but Headingley taught you to expect it."

Lawrence Booth, 27, is Wisden.com's assistant editor and main match reporter. "The last 24 hours of the Lord's Test in 2000 when England skittled West Indies for 54 and then tiptoed to victory by two wickets."

Simon Briggs, 28, is deputy cricket correspondent of the *Daily Telegraph*. He was previously features editor of *Wisden Cricket Monthly*, a rock critic and an occasional all-rounder for Oxfordshire Under-15s. "The 1999 World Cup semi-final at Edgbaston. All the ebb and flow of a good Test match, distilled into one day."

Don Cameron, 69, was cricket writer of the *New Zealand Herald* for 38 years and rugby writer for 13. Now retired, he freelances, gardens and listens to music. "The Gabba, 1985-86, when Richard Hadlee's 9 for 53 and superb catching led by Jeremy Coney set up an innings win. A stunning team performance which removed forever the Australian inference that New Zealand were country cousins."

Nigel Davies, 37, is art director of *Wisden Cricket Monthly* and *Wisden Asia Cricket*. "A Lord's Taverners match at Southgate in the '70s featuring Pikey from *Dad's Army* and Eric Morecambe with his double-width bat. Enduring image …"

Geoffrey Dean, 40, is one of the *Times's* cricket correspondents. He previously wrote for the *Daily Telegraph* and opened the bowling for county 2nd XIs. "Bridgetown, 1992, when South Africa, with eight wickets in hand on the final morning, needed 70-odd to win their first Test since readmission. Magical bowling by Ambrose and Walsh produced an astonishing victory at the end of a wonderfully entertaining match."

Steven Lynch, 44, is database director of Wisden.com and former managing editor of *Wisden Cricket Monthly*. The author of *The Lord's Test*, he also writes for the *Sunday Telegraph*. "The final day of the Ashes Test at Melbourne 1982-83. None of my family could fathom why I was off to see what might be just one ball. About 18,000 equally strange people turned up too. Border and Thommo inched Australia to within a boundary-hit of victory … and then Botham came back on."

Neil Manthorp, 34, is a commentator and writer based in Cape Town who has travelled extensively with the South African team since 1991. A founder member of the sports news agency MWP Media Sport, he contributes to the *Sunday Telegraph*, the BBC World Service and Wisden.com. "Zimbabwe's inaugural Test match against India, Harare, 1992. A team of jolly club cricketers who still changed out of their suits and farming clothes next to the nets, up against the might of India. The game was awful, but Zimbabweans can look back at that scorecard for the next 200 years and feel proud. Their team had a great sense of history and what they wanted to achieve. I don't know whether I loved it or hated it, but I won't forget it."

Mark Ray, 49, played for NSW and captained Tasmania in the 1980s before becoming a cricket writer, notably for the *Sydney Morning Herald*, and photographer. His second book of photographs will be out in November. "Chennai, 2001 – the final day of what was probably the best three-match series ever. Australia's batsmen fought desperately against Harbhajan to leave India a chase of 155. McGrath and Gillespie bowled superbly on a flat pitch in the heat and humidity in front of 60,000 roaring fans. Gillespie's last spell nearly pulled off a great win. Australia lost but still proved how good they were."

Chris Ryan, 28, is a Sydney journalist, author of Wisden.com's Australian View, and a former managing editor of *Wisden Cricket Monthly*. "My first time lingers longest: Perth, Nov 1981, Australia v Pakistan. Graham Yallop made an unremarkable 38 and Sarfraz Nawaz took an unremarkable 0 for 88, but my memory is of Kim Hughes's velvet driving and sharing bottomless bags of Minties with my Mum."

Simon Wilde, 41, has been cricket correspondent of the *Sunday Times* since 1998. He previously worked for the *Times* and *Wisden Cricket Monthly*. His fourth book, *Caught: The Full Story of Cricket's Match-Fixing Scandal*, was published to acclaim last year. "England inching to victory over West Indies on the Saturday of the Lord's Test in 2000, exhausting to watch let alone write about, but ultimately satisfying."

Index